222 Prosperity Affirmations: How to Speak Prosperity and Abundance into your life!

By Justin Perry

YouAreCreators
P.O. Box 756
Tinley Park, IL 60477

If you have read my other books, "I Wish I knew 20 Years Ago" or "The Little Book of Successful Secrets", you would know that I like to get straight to the point. I don't care for fluff and I prefer to get right into the juice. This book is no exception. If anyone knows about the power of affirmations and the "spoken word", it's me. I completely transformed my life using the techniques I'm about to show you. I went from earning $30,000 a year to now, over $350,000 by using and applying these methods. I assure you, they work and will always work. See, we are working with Universal laws and unlike the laws of men, these laws cannot be broken. These laws work whether you are young or old, black or white, rich or poor. One of these laws is known as the 'Law of Gestation'. This Universal law states that every word, thought, vision, or belief that is held continually, will eventually manifest in the physical world. What I'm about to show you is how to use this universal law to unlock the prosperity and abundance that is waiting for you. There is a goldmine in your mind and in your mouth and I'm going to show you how to let it out. This book's main focus will be about, "The Spoken Word" and how it attracts or repels prosperity.

How Do Affirmations Work?

The words you often use create tracks in your subconscious mind. The more you say them, the deeper the tracks become. Your subconscious mind is what records everything in your life, including the words you speak and the thoughts you think. Say or think a thing enough times, and it becomes a belief in the subconscious mind. Based on the

Universal Law of Belief, what you honestly believe has to eventually manifest in the outside world. Here's the kicker, you have to ingrain these beliefs with feeling, conviction, and repetition in order to have them take effect in your life. Once you mix emotions with affirmations you fuel them with enough energy to manifest in the physical world.

Anthropologist and body language expert, Raymond Birdwhistell determined in his 1970 experiment, that our self-talk has a 100% impact on the successes and failures of our life. So if you want to live a successful life, you must construct a new vocabulary that implements success. You must talk like you're already successful, even if success is nowhere in sight!

The Vibratory Power of Words

From an esoteric standpoint, the spoken "WORD" contains very powerful properties. There is a vibratory power in words. If everything is energy, your words have to be a form of energy also. What makes words so special is that once spoken, words can be felt and heard instantly by others, thus causing them to think the same thing. Words are pure vibration and based on the intention behind the words used, it can produce a constructive or destructive effect.

Many people think the word *Abracadabra* is just a fancy word used by magicians, but the origin of the word derives from an ancient Aramaic phrase which means, "I create as I speak" or "I create like the word". The same word in Hebrew translates to "It came to pass as it was spoken." Many of the ancients have long known the mystical powers of the verbalized word.

The power of the spoken word can be seen in tests like Dr. Emoto's "Water Experiment". In the "Water Experiment", Dr. Emoto filled multitude petri dishes of water (from the same source), and wrote a variety of words on each one. For example, he wrote, "I love you" on one, "You make me sick, I will kill you" on another, "You Fool" on the next, and a mixture of positive, loving words on other dishes. Every day for 30 days, he literally spoke to the petri dishes with the same intention as the words written on each dish.

He froze the water and decided to hold them under a high powered microscope. What he found blew him away...

The dishes that had positive and loving words written and spoken to them, had beautiful formations of crystals, while the dishes that contained negative words looked to be toxic and poisoned. It makes you question, if our bodies are 70% water, what effects do our words and intentions have on the health and well-being of our bodies?

What Are You Attaching to Your "I-Am"?

In ancient Jewish culture, the words "I-Am" was said to be the name of God and was considered sacred and holy. Saying the words "I-Am" was forbidden and even punishable by death. The Jewish mystics knew that words weren't simply a combination of noises, but held and contained the nature of the definition of the word spoken. Whatever you attach to "I-Am", you become. That is why I recommend you start most of your affirmations with "I-Am". Whatever you put behind the words "I-Am", becomes a part of your experience. You become that, and it becomes you. Use your "I-Am" WISELY!

The focus of this book is prosperity and financial abundance. I put emphasis on finances because the subject seems to be partially taboo. People don't want to admit how important money really is in our everyday lives. Modern society is constructed in such a way that you need money for almost EVERYTHING. Just a few necessities that cost money: Water, food, clothes, automobile, (not including gas and maintenance) rent or mortgage. And it doesn't end there, you have to pay for health insurance, car insurance, home insurance, and of course BILLS. Let's not forget taxes and more taxes… and did I mention taxes? Oh, and If you have children, you can literally double every example I just gave you. Do not fret my friend, I am going to teach you some simple techniques that will increase the cash flow in your life for the rest of your life! (Only if you make this a habit)

In order to attain this financial abundance, you have to believe that it's possible to have and that you deserve it! Many of us from an early age have been taught that we don't deserve the good things life has to offer. If you have a belief that money is evil or unclean, let's face it, you're going to have a hard time with money. Money isn't evil or unclean, it's simply a medium of exchange from services. To be technical, money is made out of the same thing as you and me. Its ENERGY! Ask any Quantum physicists, and they'll tell you, under any high powered microscope, everything is made of one thing... Energy! That also includes money.

The energy that is money can be described as one word, "observant". Money has the ability to hear and feel your opinion about it. As the late Rev Ike would say, "Think of money like a woman, if you talk bad about her, she'll want nothing to do with you!". Money has ears and is always listening. So if you're talking negative about money, claiming that money is evil, what you're doing is literally pushing money away from you.

Make Friends with Money

In order to attract money, you have to develop a positive mental attitude and feeling regarding money. You must acknowledge money for its wonderful ability to provide you with life's essentials and experiences. I like to think of money as a friend or a sidekick of mine that is closer to me then my breath. Money is my loyal assistant, ever ready to provide me with every physical desire and need that arises. Talk to money in loving ways, tell it, "We are friends, and when I give you out, you come back to me multiplied". Money isn't good, money is VERY good. Money can provide you with a roof over your head, security to pay your bills, the ability to travel the world and collect life's experiences. Not to mention, money can purchase the material goods that you've always desired.

Often times people don't want to seem materialistic, so they refuse to obtain the things that they secretly desire. What actually happens is, they set up mental road blocks in their subconscious mind that sabotages and repels the good that could be theirs. These road blocks can only be demolished by reinforcing new beliefs through repetition. Your self-talk becomes your beliefs and your beliefs create your reality.

We often forget, we came to this earth to have a **human experience**. Since we live in a material world, it only makes sense to obtain material goods in order to fulfill our human experience. But, moderation is key-- as Sandra Rodgers said in her book, "Lessons from the Light", "Everything in moderation; an overindulge in anything will cause a burden in one's life." In other words, you shouldn't be overly spiritual, and you shouldn't undermine your material impulses either. As the late Stuart Wilde once said, "You have a divine right to abundance, and if you are anything less than a millionaire, you haven't had your fair share."

I have been poor and I am now rich, and I'm here to tell you, that being rich feels much closer to my natural state of being. I don't serve money, money serves me and I am grateful for our wonderful friendship.

Visualizing Money Sticking

After years of observation and personal experience, I have become a true believer of visualization. Time and time again, I have seen the mental movies in my mind become physical manifestations over time. I like to visualize money rushing in and sticking to me. I picture it sticking until every inch of my body is covered in hundred dollar bills. Then I repeat to myself, "I am a money magnet, I am one with the energy of money!" I say this until there is an overwhelming feeling of wealth and abundance. I hold this feeling for about 70 seconds and then I release it, and let it go. Within hours or days, I start to receive money from expected and unexpected places. Think of your prosperity and abundance like a water hose that is currently circulating water, and this water hose is connected to Source/God. When we have limited beliefs or fearful feelings and thoughts about money, we literally pinch and close off the flow of our prosperity. What we need to know is, we can never fully cut ourselves off from this source. It is forever flowing and ever giving. To unblock the flow of abundance, you must nourish positive thoughts, feelings and words regarding money. Anytime you feel like your prosperity is blocked, I want you to visualize your "abundance water hose" full of lavish water supply. Nothing gets the juices back flowing like some strong wealth affirmations bathed in the feeling of authority.

Affirmations are a great way of changing your belief patterns into FEELING that you deserve the best life has to offer. I practice affirmations whenever I can, that's why I developed an app that allows you to create your own affirmations and sends them to you at random times every day. You can download our app, "YouAreCreators Manifestation Reminder", completely free in your Apple or Android app store. (Yes, that was a shameless plug).

I do my affirmations whenever I feel inspired, or whenever fear or doubt creeps into my mind. I counter fearful thoughts with empowering, positive thoughts. In the shower, I speak my good. In the car, I speak my good. Even when I'm planting my flowers, I speak my good. The vibrations of your words are either bringing you all the things you've always wanted, or they are actively repelling them; you're in the captain's seat. You can decide whether to guide your ship into the raging storm, or you can ride it into paradise. It's truly up to you. Guide your words and you'll guide your life.

Giving and Receiving

One of the greatest lessons regarding money that I have learned, is that it always has to be kept in circulation. A closed hand cannot give or receive blessings. Remember, the energy you give out is what you'll also receive. Giving money to a person in need or to a noble cause can only open your pathway to receiving more money. "Give and it is given unto you", as my friend from Galilee once said. (I know this doesn't involve "speaking wealth" into your life, but I felt guided to include it)

Words You Should Never Use with Money

Many of us have grown up saying and using words that actually pushes money away from us. We have done this innocently, but it is time to fix this simple mistake. Here are a couple of words that should never be included in a sentence with money: Spend, Waste, & Exhaust.

Let's break down those words by their definitions:

Spend - To pay out, disburse, or expend; dispose of (money)

Waste - To consume, spend, or employ uselessly or without adequate return; use to no avail or profit; squander

Exhaust- To use up or consume completely; expend the whole of.

These words have negative implications and if used enough times; becomes associated subconsciously with your ideas regarding money.

Instead of using words like "Spend, Waste & Exhaust", try substituting them with the words "Use" or "Circulate". When something is circulated, it leaves, but eventually returns back to its state of origin. (I learned this wonderful lesson from the late great Rev Ike)

Enough with the chatter, let's get to the actual affirmations. You'll notice that all 222 affirmations have a "!" behind them because they are meant to be spoken with intense emotion and strong feelings. Say these affirmations so often that they begin to roll off your tongue. Habits are built through repetition, so say these whenever possible. It takes 15 to 40 days to form a brand new habit. These new habits will completely change your financial future but you must be committed.

If you go to my website, "youarecreators.org" you can print these affirmations up for free (In the "Free download" section). After you print them, hang them in your bathroom right next to your toilet. While you're doing your business on the toilet, you can look over and speak your finances into existence!

These are the prosperity affirmations that I use every single day! Some of these are my personal affirmations that were created by me, while others are affirmations that I gathered from certain websites that I have adopted in my daily routine. (Websites provided in back credits)

Say each affirmation with FEELING AND AUTHORITY!

COMMAND AND DEMAND YOUR GOOD!

(Say at least 20 of these affirmations every single day!)

1. I am a prosperity magnet!

2. The energy of money is always drawn to me!

3. I am a prosperity powerhouse!

4. Money is a wonderful friend of mine, and we are always together!

5. All things lead to my prosperity, and wealth!

6. I am one with _____ (amount of dollars that you want)

7. My bank account is always filled with money!

8. Money comes to me easily and effortlessly!

9. I attract money naturally!

10. A constant flow of money comes to me from known and unknown sources!

11. I attract money everywhere I go!

12. I always have more money coming in than going out!

13. As I do what I love, money flows freely to me!

14. I now attract opportunities to effortlessly make money!

15. I am supposed to be rich, I am supposed to be wealthy!

16. All the money I need is flowing to me now!

17. Whatever I do attract me more money!

18. I am Rich, I am Prosperous, I am Abundant!

19. I love the energy of money!

20. Every day I am attracting and saving more and more money!

21. I have more money than I know what to do with!

22. I have more money than I ever dreamed possible!

23. Earning and receiving money comes naturally to me!

24. I am supposed to be financially rich, it's by birthright!

25. My vibration is always attuned to wealth!

26. I believe in my ability to manifest an abundance of money!

27. I am always connected to the energy of money!

28. Wealth, prosperity, and abundance are always in the back of my mind!

29. I deserve all prosperity of all kinds!

30. I draw prosperity of all kinds to me now!

31. I am a money magnet!

32. I'm always open to receiving money!

33. I am tapped into the universal supply of money!

34. Money is all around me!

35. When I use money, money comes back to me multiplied!

36. I am unlimited when it comes to wealth and prosperity!

37. Money comes to me easily and frequently!

38. I always have a lot of money in the bank!

39. Money is wonderful stuff!

40. I have over 7 sources of passive income!

41. I am a money Master!

42. I am a master of wealth!

43. I manage money wisely!

44. I always have more than enough money!

45. I am wealthy!

46. I am affluent!

47. I am rich!

48. I have an endless supply of money!

49. Money comes to me in all kinds of ways!

50. Money is constantly pouring into my life!

51. Prosperity is my natural vibration!

52. I have more money than I know what to do with!

53. I am unlimited when it comes to wealth and prosperity!

54. I earn money just by breathing!

55. My life is an example of prosperity in its highest form!

56. I'm ultra-successful!

57. Successful money-making ideas are always entering my mind!

58. Prosperity should be my middle name!

59. I am Lucky, I am fortunate, I am blessed when it comes to prosperity!

60. Money is good and money is my friend!

61. I attract Prosperity wealth and abundance at every turn!

62. Money comes to me from expected and unexpected sources!

63. Wealth-- it's always in the back of my mind!

64. My income is constantly increasing!

65. I earn and receive more money every single day!

66. Wealth and abundance is my natural state of being!

67. Money is attracted to me and I am attracted to money!

68. My life is overflowing with God's lavish abundance!

69. I have more money than I ever dreamed possible!

70. I always have enough money to share and to spare!

71. I am magnificent at earning passive income!

72. I am financially secure I am financially independent!

73. I'm supposed to be rich I'm supposed to be wealthy!

74. I am open and receptive to all the wealth life offers me!

75. I welcome an unlimited source of income and wealth in my life!

76. I use money to better my life and the lives of others!

77. I am aligned with the energy of abundance!

78. Money impacts my life in positive ways!

79. I constantly attract opportunities that creates money!

80. I always have more money than what I need!

81. The Universe is the constant supplier of money for me!

82. I am great with money!

83. I am fully supported making money doing what I love to do!

84. Abundance and I are one!

85. I expect lavish abundance!

86. All I have to do is ask for abundance and allow it!

87. I allow my income to constantly expand and I always live in comfort and joy!

88. I attract money everywhere I go!

89. I accept all the joy and prosperity life has to offer!

90. All the money I need is flowing to me now!

91. The more money I have, the more money I have to give!

92. Money is always circulating freely in my life and there is always a surplus!

93. All my bills are paid with wonderful ease!

94. I always circulate money in my life!

95. I am boundless abundance!

96. I am connected to the natural flow of abundance!

97. Wealth is within me, wealth in around me!

98. Every day and in every way, I get attract more and more wealth!

99. I'm supposed to be rich, I am supposed to be wealthy!

100. With every breathe I take, I attract more and more wealth to me!

101. Money loves to be around me!

102. Money sticks to me like feathers stick to glue!

103. Wealth ideas are always entering my mind!

104. I allow prosperity into my life!

105. I am one with a tremendous amount of money!

106. I am a magnet of success and good fortune!

107. I live in a Universe of Abundance!

108. My wallet is always overflowing with money!

109. I am open and receptive to new avenues of income!

110. The Universe is a constant supplier of money and I have always had more than enough to fulfill all my needs!

111. I release all resistance to money and I now allow it to flow easily to me!

112. Money is not an object but an energy that I am attracting every moment of my life!

113. All my needs and desires are met even before I ask!

114. I know there is plenty for all of us!

115. There is always abundance of money available to me!

116. My good comes from everywhere and everyone!

117. I use the money to do meaningful things and give myself the best in life!

118. There is always abundance of money available to me!

119. Money is an integral part of my life and it is always attached to me!

120. Everything I touch turns into gold!

121. I have more riches than I asked for!

122. I am receiving money making ideas every day!

123. I am always receiving unexpected checks in the mail!

124. I am attracting more and more money from multiple sources now!

125. I love money and money love me back!

126. I FEEL Rich!

127. I love money, and money loves me!

128. I am abundant in all positive areas of life!

129. Every day my money consciousness is increasing and keeping me surrounded by money!

130. Money is flowing to me like a river!

131. I create money and abundance through Joy and Self-love!

132. Subconsciously I love money and money flow easily into my life!

133. I attract money everywhere I go!

134. I live in a Universe of Abundance!

135. I am bountifully supplied with money!

136. I accept all the joy and prosperity life has to offer!

137. Financial success comes to me easily and effortlessly!

138. My income always exceeds my expenses!

139. My grateful heart is a magnet that attracts more of everything I desire!

140. I have a positive money mindset!

141. Attracting money is easy!

142. Everything I touch is a success!

143. Prosperity is drawn to me wherever I go!

144. Wealth is good, wealth is amazing!

145. Money is a wonderful example of service and ideas!

146. Money is a good friend of mine; we are very close!

147. Wealth, abundance, prosperity and opulence is mine!

148. Wealth and abundance is the only state of being that I accept!

149. I'm supposed to be prosperous, I'm supposed to be rich!

150. The source of the universe is rich and opulence, therefore so am I!

151. The more positive attention I give to wealth; the more wealth I attract!

152. Money is energy, and I am filled with the energy of money!

153. My thoughts are always attuned to wealth and abundance!

154. I have the ability to be as successful as I want to be!

155. I trust that I am always guided to obtain prosperity!

156. I am intuitively guided to wealth and prosperity!

157. The more money I attain; the more opportunities I seem to attract!

158. I am the king/queen of passive income!

159. I am a master of finance!

160. I always have loads of disposable income!

161. God/The Universe is my source of supply; therefore, I am unlimited!

162. The more money I have, the more service I can provide to the masses!

163. I choose my life, so I CHOOSE to be wealthy!

164. I love paying all my bills on time!

165. I am grateful for all my multiple streams of income!

166. The more gratitude I feel; the more prosperity I attain!

167. I was prosperous, am prosperous and will always be prosperous!

168. I always have whatever I need. The Universe takes good care of me!

169. I am a magnet for money. Prosperity of every kind is drawn to me!

170. I love prosperity and I attract it naturally!

171. My income is constantly increasing and I prosper wherever I turn!

172. I spend/circulate money under direct inspiration wisely and fearlessly, knowing my supply is endless and immediate!

173. I am fearless in letting money go out, knowing God is my immediate and endless supply!

174. I now release the gold-mine within me. I am linked with an endless golden stream of prosperity which comes to me under grace in perfect ways!

175. Every day in every way I am becoming more prosperous!

176. I am open and receptive to all the abundance in the universe!

177. My financial abundance overflows today!

178. I was destined to be prosperous. I have abundance to share and spare!

179. Every day in every way, my wealth is increasing!

180. I am thankful for the abundance and prosperity in my life!

181. Today is rich with opportunities and I open my heart to receive them!

182. My attitude towards money is becoming more positive with each day!

183. I deserve to be wealthy and have financial freedom!

184. I find it easy to think positively about money!

185. Each day I am becoming more and more financially healthy!

186. I am a master at investing my money!

187. My financial investments are always doubling!

188. Every day in every way, my wealth is increasing!

189. Financial opportunities are always arriving in my life!

190. Abundance within me, abundance around me!

191. Every day is a wealthy day!

192. Every day I am attracting and saving more and more money!

193. I see myself as Prosperous, now! God/The Universe gives to me rich, lavish financial blessings now!

194. New opportunities to increase my income open up for me now!

195. I consistently and easily manifest the money I desire to live my dreams!

196. I now make a fortune doing what I love!

197. I now give and receive more freely!

198. I have a continuous abundance of prosperity flowing to me always!

199. My finances are divinely blessed!

200. I now attract incredible opportunities to increase the wealth in my life!

201. I now get divine wisdom on financial matters!

202. I see and construct prosperity. I see myself deserving it. I am open to it!

203. I know that life is abundant and I accept abundance in my life now!

204. I will visualize myself open and receptive to all wealth!

205. I envision complete abundance and I visualize myself open and receptive to all wealth!

206. I see wealth coming effortlessly and easily to me!

207. I enlarge my prosperity consciousness and THINK BIG!

208. I see and construct prosperity easily and effortlessly!

209. The more grateful I am; the more reasons I find to be grateful!

210. I construct wealth easily!

211. I am fearless in letting money go out, knowing God/ The Universe is my immediate and endless supply!

212. I prosper in health. I prosper in finances. I prosper in love. I prosper in peace!

213. I awake each morning excited to pursue my passion which provides generous financial prosperity!

214. I deserve prosperity, and I accept prosperity in my life!

215. I attract prosperity with each thought I think!

216. I know that the world is prosperous. I notice prosperity all around me!

217. Thank you for my prosperity, I will prosper for the rest of my days!

218. Wealth seems to follow me wherever I go!

219. Money is the easiest thing to make!

220. Prosperity is my way of life!

221. Money always seems to fall in my lap!

222. Wealth, abundance and prosperity, are infinitely provided for me!

   Say these affirmations as often as you can, with as much feeling as you can, and watch how your life begins to change!

Inserting these affirmations to your daily routine will surly increase the amount of prosperity in your life. Give it 30 days, and watch how your life begins to reflect abundance and prosperity.

It has been my pleasure to provide you with this ancient knowledge and new understanding. This is Justin from YouAreCreators, and we support your dreams!

Affirmation sources and a special thank you to:

www.awesomeaj.com
www.powerfulmoneyaffirmations.com
www.yes-icandoit.com
www.seedsofprosperity.com
www.affirmationpower.com

Made in the USA
Las Vegas, NV
24 July 2022